DANGER ZONE

Held to Ransom

by ANTHONY MASTERS

Illustrated by Tim Sell

EDGE

FRANKLIN WATTS

LONDON·SY

D1078722

This edition 2010

Franklin Watts
338 Euston Road
London
NW1 3BH

Franklin Watts Australia
Level 17/207 Kent Street
Sydney NSW 2000

Cover design: Peter Scoulding

Cover image: Stockphoto4u/iStockphoto

A CIP catalogue record for
this book is available from
the British Library.

ISBN: 978 0 7496 9492 0

Dewey Classification: 364.1'54'092

10 9 8 7 6 5 4 3 2 1

Printed in Great Britain

Franklin Watts is a division of Hachette Children's Books,
an Hachette UK company.

www.hachette.co.uk

Contents

DANGER ZONE
FACT FILE

LOCATION

Near Rome
in Italy

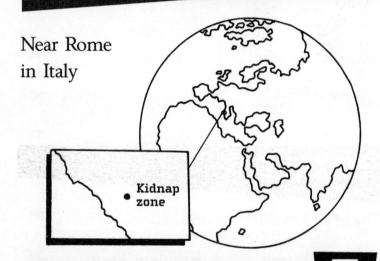

Kidnap
zone

DANGER

Kidnap victim might be murdered

PERSONNEL

Nicola Brunelli

HAZARDS

! Nicola might not be released, even if ransom paid
! More money could be demanded and Nicola still might not be released
! John Seton, security adviser, could make a mistake and annoy the gang - this could result in Nicola's murder
! Nicola might fall ill
! Nicola's spirit could be broken

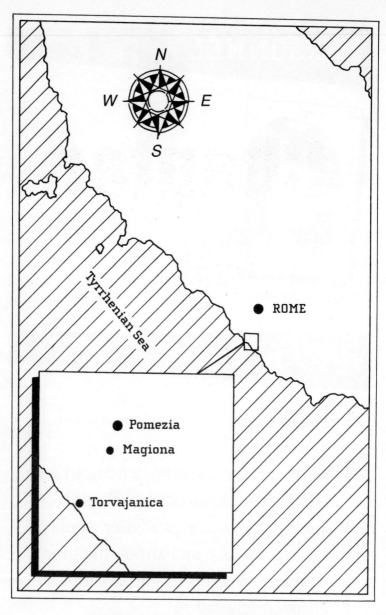

Map showing area where
Nicola Brunelli was held

Chapter One

Shocked!
Friday July 17th, 1981 – 11.45pm

Nicola Brunelli hurried back to the hotel that was owned by her family. They had forgotten the key to their seaside chalet.

Nicola said that she would go back and get it.

As she returned, she ran straight into the arms of her kidnappers. They had been waiting for her in an Alfa Romeo parked close by.

■ Knocked-down

Although she was only thirteen, Nicola was tall and strong. Her four kidnappers grabbed her by the arms and legs. She managed to kick one of the men and knock him down.

The other three carried her to the car. A pistol shot was fired as the car roared away. This was a warning.

It showed that the gang meant business. No rescue should be attempted.

■ Handcuffed

Three minutes later, the Alfa Romeo skidded to a halt. The gang put tape over Nicola's eyes and ears. They dragged her into another car and handcuffed her.

The more Nicola struggled, the more the handcuffs tightened round her wrists.

She was so shocked she could hardly understand what was happening.

Chapter Two

The Kidnapping Crime

Nicola was kidnapped from the *Centre Brunelli*. This was a seaside complex that was owned by her family.

The Brunellis were well-known and respected. They owned other hotels. They were very rich.

Kidnapping in Italy had become a major and repeated crime. The police were working hard to put an end to snatches with high ransom demands.

▪ Shots in the air

Only a few months before, an attempted
kidnap had been made on Nicola's brother.
The gang had broken his car's windscreen
with the butt of a revolver. Hearing his son's
screams, his father had run out firing his gun.

The gang had panicked and run off.

This was a clear warning to the Brunelli family. They were now kidnap targets.

But in spite of this, the family did not have bodyguards for their children.

■ Close by

As a result, the gang tried again. Nicola was taken. Her brother was close by, sitting in his car talking to friends. But the kidnap was so quick he stood no chance of saving his sister.

Chapter Three

Blindfolded

Nicola was driven for about twenty minutes. She was tied up, with her eyes and ears taped for the whole time. She was taken to a house in the country.

But Nicola spent her first night in the back of the car.

She kept telling her kidnappers that her father was ill. They told her not to worry and that soon everything would be all over.

She was very worried about the meaning of those words. Were the kidnappers going to kill her?

■ Powerful people

The next morning, Nicola was blindfolded and taken to another house. She was only kept there for a day.

She knew the police were active in the area. She could hear sirens. Nicola prayed they would find her quickly.

She knew her family were powerful people in Italy and would do everything they could to get her back.

Chapter Four

A Ransom Demand

Six days passed. Nicola's family still had not heard from her. The Brunelli family was desperate with worry.

The family knew they couldn't go to the police. They decided to employ a British security adviser called John Seton. He was experienced in negotiating with kidnappers.

▪ A coded message

Seton told the family to place a coded message in a local newspaper. It read 'Sea bass on the menu today at our previous price'.

This was meant to worry the gang. The real kidnappers had still not made contact. Seton wanted them to think that the family had started negotiating with another group.

He hoped that the real gang would contact the family, afraid that the 'hoaxers' might get the money the kidnappers saw as theirs.

■ A letter

On July 28th, just before the message appeared in the Italian newspaper, *Il Messaggero*, a letter arrived from Nicola. It was addressed to her parents.

Part of it read:

When I think that you're suffering because of me, especially Papa who is very ill, I feel like I'm dying. I don't think it's a good idea to describe the conditions I'm being kept in... I've been told that for my release we need 7000 million lire.

▪ Inside information?

Was it a coincidence that the kidnappers' contact came just before the Brunellis' message appeared in the paper? Or did they have inside information from the newspaper?

Nicola went on to tell her parents to put an advertisement in *Il Messaggero*. It should say, 'LOST CANARY IN TORVAJANICA, GREEN EYES, BIG REWARD'.

▪ Ready to pay

This message would tell the kidnappers the family was ready to pay.

The gang would then reply with the message, 'THE SEA IS WARM TO BATHE IN'.

Chapter Five

The Kidnap Business

On July 29th, 1981, another letter arrived from Nicola. It was sent to Marcello Brunelli, one of her uncles.

The kidnappers have allowed me to write a letter to Mama and Papa. In the letter, I have given the instructions for my release and how contact is to be made. Every day passes slowly and... I cannot see when I will return home.

▪ Budget

Seton knew from the letters that he was dealing with a gang who were very experienced in the kidnap business.

He thought that the Brunelli family must budget for paying a ransom of between 700 and 800 million lire (£350-£400,000).

Seton advised the family to make a first payment offer. The family agreed.

They placed the advertisement to show that they were ready to make a payment.

■ Turned down

At 9.02 pm on July 30th, 1981, the family was contacted by the gang. Their first ransom offer of 280 million lire (£140,000) was turned down.

The kidnappers were angry. The ransom offer was too little. They told the Brunelli family to contact them when they were ready with a larger amount of money.

Seton reckoned the gang would try to get a first payment.

And then a second!

Chapter Six

Held to Ransom

The complicated negotiations continued for the next three months. During this period, Nicola was moved five times by her kidnappers.

At first, she was kept in a tent inside a room. The tent was near a kitchen, but she hardly ever had any hot food.

■ No appetite

She ate mainly tinned tomatoes, tinned tuna fish, Philadelphia cream cheese, or ham. Sometimes she was given pastries, chocolate, pizza, biscuits or scrambled and boiled eggs.

Nicola didn't have much appetite.

■ Chained

For the first three days, the kidnappers cruelly kept the tape over Nicola's eyes.

When they eventually took it off, it was several days before she could see again.

Nicola's wrists remained badly bruised by the handcuffs for some time. Her hands and feet were chained to heavy lumps of concrete.

Nicola had only a mattress for a bed. She was given a portable toilet, but it was only emptied every few days.

Although she only spoke to two or three members of the gang, Nicola realised there were many others.

Chapter
Seven

Punished

During the first month, Nicola hoped every day that she would be freed.

Each time she asked them, a gang member told her, 'We have called your family and tomorrow you'll be going home.'

This was said so many times that it became a special torture.

■ A plan

Meanwhile, John Seton was trying to get the gang to think that the Brunelli family had less money than they had thought. He worked out a plan.

The family should try to sell one of its four restaurants to raise cash for the ransom. The staff would then protest against the sale.

The press could then report the family were trying to raise the money, but had a problem with the staff.

This was one of several ideas Seton suggested to show how 'poor' the family was.

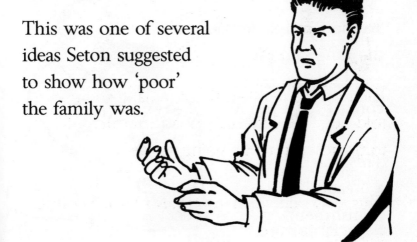

When the gang next made contact, the Brunellis increased their ransom offer to 450 million lire (£225,000).

The kidnappers turned the offer down again. They told the family that if they didn't have enough money, they should get a bank loan.

On Saturday 22nd August, the thirty-sixth day of Nicola's kidnap, the gang called to say they were not happy with the way things were going.

■ Despair

To the family's despair, the gang said there would be no more contact for a month.

This was a dreadful punishment.

Chapter
Eight

A Payment Drop

After some time, negotiations over Nicola's ransom began again. But, by now, the family was being questioned by the police.

They were putting pressure on the family to trace the kidnappers.

An Italian judge tried to get the banks to report if money was withdrawn from the Brunellis' account. He wanted to stop a payment being made to the kidnappers.

■ A new demand

But, on September 20th, 1981, sixty-five days after Nicola had been taken, a payment of 800 million lire was made.

To the family's horror, Alphonso, the gang's negotiator, immediately demanded a further 900 million lire (£450,000).

Shortly after the second demand, a letter arrived from Nicola pleading for help:

> If you don't make another payment, you may never see me again.

▪ Lost dog

In the same envelope there was also a letter from her kidnappers. They told the Brunellis to place a new advert when they could pay the money. It should read:

'Lost dog – Poodle, white, Villa Pamphili, Big Reward.'

Put your advertisement, in the paper ONLY WHEN you are sure you can meet our demands. We want 900 million lire. We will not take any notice of your excuses such as poor health.

Chapter Nine

A Chance Escape

The negotiations dragged on.

Then, one hundred days after Nicola's kidnap, the Brunelli family received a call from the police.

Nicola had been rescued.

■ Wanted criminal

The police had been tracking a wanted criminal, De Sanctis, whom they believed to be involved in recent kidnappings.

De Sanctis *was* involved: he was the leader of the gang who had kidnapped Nicola. He had been spotted by the police.

In a dramatic chase, De Sanctis had been shot in the arm.

Injured, he had hidden in the villa where Nicola was kept. The rest of the gang fled, fearing they would be discovered. Nicola was alone with De Sanctis.

And now De Sanctis was cornered.

■ Turned away

Nicola had never seen the faces of her kidnappers. Now she faced De Sanctis. Nicola turned away.

She was frightened that he would kill her if she saw his face. But De Sanctis told Nicola her kidnap was over.

▪ Overpowered

The police had surrounded the house. Nicola heard shots.

The police broke in to find De Sanctis holding Nicola in front of him. He was using her as a shield. But he was quickly overpowered.

Nicola was very weak.

She had been kept in a wooden box, with her legs chained. She was now free, but unable to walk. The police carried her out.

▪ Reunited

Still with chains on her legs, Nicola was taken to police headquarters in Rome. Here, she was reunited with her parents.

Speaking about her ordeal some years later, Nicola said, 'I thought they wanted to kill me. I was sure of that.'

She was probably right. If the police hadn't been lucky, Nicola would most likely have been killed.

Further Facts

- Kidnappers often keep quiet for a long time after they have made the snatch. This makes sure the family is put under terrible stress. They wonder what has happened and if the victim is still alive. The family also wonder how much money the gang will ask for the release of their loved one.

- This 'softening-up' process is a well-known tactic. Kidnappers like to negotiate when the family is at its weakest. The gang wants to try to keep the police out of the negotiations. They want to be in control.

- Kidnapping in Italy happened often in the 1970s and 1980s. The police and the law courts were determined to put a stop to it. They tried to prevent payments from being made. They hoped that gangs would stop kidnapping when they knew that the victim's family did not control its own money.

- The Brunelli family had brought in a security adviser who had plenty of experience with kidnappers. He stood the best chance of negotiating with them.

- Many gangs let the victims' families think that they would take the first payment and that would be all. But then they would keep their victim and ask for a second payment.

Glossary

Budget: A plan for spending money.

Coincidence: When similar things happen by chance.

Criminal: Someone who breaks the law.

Hoaxers: People who play a trick on others to fool them.

Kidnappers: Gangs who take people and ask for money in order for the victims to be returned.

Lire: Italian money.

Negotiations: Talks to try and reach a deal.

Punishment: An action carried out to make someone suffer for doing something wrong.

Ransom: The amount of money demanded in order for the victim to be released.

Security adviser: An expert on safety.

Shield: To protect.

Important Dates

1981

July 17th	Nicola Brunelli kidnapped.
July 23rd	Security adviser employed by family.
July 28th-29th	Letters arrive from Nicola to family.
July 30th	Coded message from family to kidnappers placed in press.
July 30th	Gang contact family to turn down ransom offer.
August 22nd	Gang still not happy with negotiations.
September 20th	Ransom drop made. Later, more money is demanded.
October 24th	Nicola discovered in a villa near Magiona in a raid by police.